The Pizza Oven Handbook
A practical guide to building your own wood-fired oven
1st Edition

by
Andrew Thompson

www.thepizzaovenhandbook.com

Copyright

Thanks

Behind every hand-built pizza oven is a supportive family, waiting to eat pizza! To my wife and daughters who allowed me to set out on and complete this journey, thank you from the bottom of my cheesy heart.

To Cousin Matthew (Alfie) you were the best concrete mixing gaffer an oven-builder could hope for and you gave me the confidence in the beginning to forge on alone.

To Uncle Simon, I thank you for mucking in and getting your hands dirty like a true friend.

To everyone else, thank you for your support and encouragement throughout.

Andy.

Disclaimer

Please note that the information contained in this book is intended as a starting point towards building your own oven. The writer is neither a builder nor a professional in this field and the advice offered in the following pages has been collated from personal experience and research. No expert advice has been sought at any time in compiling this book.

A wood-fired oven uses both combustible and non-combustible materials and you should always seek additional guidance and advice in respect of any aspect of the build that you are unsure of or which has the potential to cause harm to you or those around you.

Consideration should be given to local and national building codes and restrictions in respect of any project of this nature, in order to ensure adherence to planning, environmental and other such laws.

Hazardous materials are used during the construction of a wood-fired oven and you should ensure that you read and understand the further warning at the start of this book for the safety of you and others.

The writer accepts no Liability for any damage, injury or loss caused as a result of any advice or information contained within this book, which is presented as a documented account of the writer's own oven build, to include tips and suggestions learned through the experience.

WARNING
Please read before continuing

It is important that you understand that working with the materials described in this book can be hazardous. Cutting firebricks and mixing 'homebrew' (described in later chapters) can create fine dust that can be harmful if breathed in. It is therefore strongly recommended that a good filtered respirator, eye protection in the form of goggles and gloves be worn when mixing/cutting/handling these ingredients/materials.

Particular care and caution should be exercised when handling or mixing LIME, which can cause severe skin irritation, chemical burns, blindness and lung damage. It is therefore important not to allow lime to come into contact with your skin, eyes or be breathed in. Eye protection, a respirator and thick rubber gloves should be warn when mixing and working with homebrew, ensuring that any exposed skin is also covered. You are advised to always read the label, warnings and COSHH information of any of the products mentioned in this book before attempting to work with them. If in doubt, seek further advice from the manufacturer or supplier.

Contents

FOREWARD

Pizza ovens or wood fired ovens have grown in popularity in recent years and they continue to do so. Why? Because they are simply amazing things to own and be able to cook all manner of dishes with.

Get them screaming hot and watch homemade pizza literally cook before your eyes, enticing you with the smell of an Italian restaurant in your own home or back garden. Let the flames die down and the oven cool a little and you are ready for roasting and grilling an array of meat, fish and vegetables.

As the oven temperature drops further, slide in some breads or even a desert. Overnight roasting large joints of meat, simply with the heat retained in the bricks after the fire has gone out. The possibilities are literally endless. However, the difference in using an open fire to cook with as opposed to gas or electric is truly an amazing experience.

A few years ago, I became obsessed with the idea of having one of these ovens in my own garden but I knew I didn't just want to buy an oven. I wanted to build one myself. Having no previous experience of building anything made from bricks and having never even mixed concrete before it was a steep learning curve though. It also required lots of research to understand how to build such an oven in a way that it would actually work as well as not fall down! In 2017 all of the hard work and determination paid off when I finally cooked my first food in the oven and no, it wasn't a pizza! It was actually a single fillet of salmon and a tray of roasted potatoes. Such a simple dish gave me the most amazing sense of achievement.

Of course I went on to cook many different things in the oven, including pizza and it lead to me helping others with building their ovens, drawing on all of the research that I had undertaken and having successfully built my own wood-fired oven. Taking all of this information, I decided to set it all out in a clear, easy to read book that anyone could pick up and apply to their own dream of building a wood fired oven for themselves. As with any project like this, there is always an opportunity to be creative, both in terms of the materials you use and the way in which you construct your oven. Size, style, shape, colour and so forth.

My aim in the following pages though is simply to set out the fundamental basics of putting together an oven in a clear and simple way that anyone with a little basic DIY knowledge can understand and apply. If you take the leap and build your own oven, hopefully it will bring you as much joy and entertainment as my oven has for my family and I.

Chapter 1

'Can I actually build a pizza oven myself?'

I went over this question time and time again before starting with this project. I had never even laid a brick or attempted to mix concrete so how would I manage not only tackling this for the first time, but with the added pressure of the finished item being capable of supporting itself, whilst containing fires hotter than a domestic oven and cooking food that I and others would eat! It seemed quite a challenge and not one that I felt confident about in the beginning to be honest.

Would this all be just a huge waste of time and money?

The more I thought about it though, the more those nagging worries started to be pushed to one side. Yes this would be difficult but what if I managed it? What if I actually managed to pull this off and build my very own brick pizza oven? Making and stretching the dough in the kitchen before taking it outside and watching it cook in little more than two minutes right before my eyes!

It was too much to resist, I had to at least try and to be honest I never looked back from that point. I had already long-since decided where the oven would go in the garden and one Sunday I just set about clearing the ground and marking out the foundation.

So do you have it in you to take on the challenge? My guess is that you do. Each step simply leads to the next and if you hit a challenge, you simply scratch your head around it until you discover or work out a solution. It really is as straightforward as that really. Take your time with each step and enjoy the journey as well as the end result.

Time

Ok, so if you are taking on this project as a builder or tradesperson then the various elements of the build are likely to progress swiftly. Conversely, the least experience you have, the longer it is going to take you to build the oven but so what? My oven was built over a couple of years off and on. Sometimes I had the time to work on it, other times I was simply too busy with other things but the project kept moving forward nevertheless. So don't worry if time is in short supply for you, simply think of the project as a number of smaller DIY-type tasks that can be undertaken individually if needs be.

Concrete curing times and the weather will also impact on the overall build time. Yes you can technically build in the rain, snow and cold but I drew the line and kept to fair-weather construction only. Generally!

Materials

Throughout this guide, I will refer to the materials that I have used. Feel free to adopt the same or similar items but at the same time don't be afraid to think outside the box with how you construct your own oven. People will have all sorts of different ideas as to what materials to use to construct the base, the hearth, the dome, the entrance, the chimney – practically everything! Decide what works for you in this regard, both within your budget and in terms of what you are able to source second hand perhaps. Just give consideration to whether the items you wish to use are strong enough and/or sufficiently heat resistant, depending on where they will feature in the build. Be creative, but safe.

Cost

So what is all this going to cost? Well, the truth is you can usually tailor your budget to fit your build. Materials are available to buy new but they are also able to be sourced through platforms such as Gumtree, Ebay and so forth. Second hand fire bricks for example can be sourced at a reduced cost, reclaimed building bricks even items discarded by others have been known to be put to good up-cycled use as chimneys, general construction or decorative finishes.

If costs are still a concern, you could consider gathering some or all of the materials over time first, before getting underway with the build. Alternatively, why not simply progress with the build slowly, as and when money and materials become available to you?

Chapter 2
Elements of an oven

Understanding the various elements of the oven will make things easier as we go on through the chapters in this book. The numbers in the above photograph correspond to the list below and set out these key components:

1. The Flue or Chimney- This is where the smoke from the fire goes. More than that though, the chimney actually helps the fire to burn efficiently. For an oven of the size shown, a flue of around 1m is recommended.

2. The Dome- The main body of the oven. Inside here is where the fire sits and where the food will be cooked.

3. The Entrance- The opening of the oven, typically a single or combination of arches.

4. Landing area- Cookware can be placed here before sliding it into the oven. Similarly, the cookware can be dragged from the oven into this area in order to check on food, turn meats or remove them from the oven when cooked.

5. The Hearth 'slab'- A platform that supports the oven itself, which usually contains insulation in order to prevent the heat from the oven escaping down.

6. The Base- This is simply to bring the oven up to a height that we can use it at. it can be made in a number of ways but is most commonly constructed of brick or breeze block.

7. The Foundation 'slab'- This supports the heavy weight of the entire oven and the all of the other components. Without this, the oven would likely sink into the ground, become unstable and possibly break or crack.

8. Wood storage area- A nice, handy way to store logs and use the space underneath the oven for tools and so forth.

Chapter 3
Foundation

The location of your oven will need some consideration. Factors to think about fall into three categories really. First and foremost is safety. When constructed properly, the fire will be contained in the oven and the exterior will become only moderately warm. Even so, citing it a reasonable distance from combustible materials such as trees and fences is sensible. Next to think about is how practical the oven's location is. The fire itself will require some monitoring and tending to from time to time, particularly when first lit. Also, whilst some dishes can be left to slowly blip away, others such as pizza will cook fast and if the oven is situated too far from the house, all that walking backwards and forwards could become tiresome. Finally, give some consideration to how the oven will look in the garden or outdoor space. Unlike a BBQ that can be put away, your oven will be on display all of the time and so needs to look good wherever it is installed. In the middle of the garden can be a great centerpiece during a pizza party but could stick out like a sore thumb during the autumn months or the depths of winter.

Once you have decided on a location, it's time to get to work mapping out the foundation that you will need to lay. This is the concrete base that we will build the base of the oven on together with anything else you wish to incorporate into the build, such as a separate worktop, BBQ etc. It is therefore important to really take the time to plan what you want in the build. Better to incorporate it into one foundation now than to try and bolt on an additional element later down the line.

At this point, you will also need to have a think about the size of the oven you wish to build. Some oven builders will set these figures in stone but I think it is more practical to allow yourself to be a little flexible in this regard. This is because when you come to build the final dome, you may find that because of the size of the bricks you have selected, going slightly under or over your planned oven size will allow you to start the first row with complete bricks, removing the need for fiddly cuts just to match your original oven size plan.

Having said that, we still need to have a figure in mind. The oven that you will see in this book has an internal diameter of around 915mm (36 inches), which means that the cooking floor inside the oven is 915mm wide. When you are planning your foundation and base, you will need to take whatever internal diameter you choose and estimate the extra room that you will need for the walls, insulation and finish of your oven. This will depend on the size of bricks that you use for the walls and also your choice/thickness of insulation.

Reading through this guide fully will hopefully allow you to build up a clear picture of the size of the base and therefore the foundation you need to construct. The table on the next page sets out an example of how you would calculate the size of the base and foundation for a 915mm oven. Some items are doubled because you need to allow for them on either side of your dome. You could of course go smaller than this but I would not recommend going too much larger for general domestic use. At 915mm you will easily fit in three or four pizzas at a time or a handful of roast meats and side dishes. If it helps, draw or chalk out a circle for your cooking floor, grab some cookware and physically see what will fit inside, remembering that you will also have a fire or burning embers in there too. Also think about whether you will just be cooking pizza or if you think you may want to venture into cooking other things? If space and cost are a factor by all means go for a smaller size, just have a good think about the above points during this planning phase of your build.

	Thickness	Total
Cooking floor diameter	915mm	915mm
Brick walls	64mm x 2	128mm
Insulation blanket	40mm x 2	80mm
Vermicrete	50mm x 2	100mm
Finishing layer (render)	10mm x 2	20mm
Dome edge to Hearth edge	50mm x 2	100mm

Adding up the final column totals 1343mm which is just over 1.3 meters and so this will be the size of your base from left to right. This same calculation can be used to work out the size of your base from front to back but you will of course need to add on whatever extra you intend to add for your oven entrance and landing area.

This comes down to personal preference and design and so searching online for ideas can really help. Of course, the table above is only shown as a guide and it will be for you to work out your own measurements base on your materials and design idea. Once you have determined your oven and base size, your foundation size follows on for this. The base walls can be built right on the edge of your foundation slab but I would recommend making your foundation slab slightly bigger than your base if possible.

An allowance for any additional items such as BBQs will also need to be added to the size and shape of your oven foundation slab because it is best to cast the foundation slab as one piece for the whole project to sit on. At this stage, it is also a good idea to think about what you will build you base out of? For instance, you may discover that if you make your foundation slightly bigger, you will be able to fit on a certain number of full-sized bricks or blocks to save you having to make awkward cuts later on.

The area for the foundation slab will need to be dug out to at least 150mm. You will then need to build a timber frame as shown in the photograph, which should sit square and level - keep checking this right up until your start pouring concrete in, just to make sure everything is really level. Use pegs if you need to in order to keep everything from moving. The top of this wooden frame will be where the top of your concrete will be so make sure it is correct at this stage.

Different schools of thought at this stage add both pea gravel and/or a damp proof membrane before pouring the concrete. I added both but whether it has/will make a significant difference to the lifespan of the project, only time will tell. Either way, it is worth setting some raised, reinforced mesh or bars within the wooden frame, which will become buried when the concrete is poured and will add to the strength of the slab. The following photograph shows what this looks like. Note: I decided to add some small gravel and a membrane to the foundation slab, which you may see in subsequent photographs.

Time to get mixing. Concrete that is. If you can hire or borrow a mixer, great but if not don't worry, you can mix these quantities by hand, just allow yourself enough time.

The mix ratio I would suggest is 1:3:6. That is one shovel of cement to three builders sand and 6 stone (small stones). If you are working with ballast, which is a mix of sand and stone then obviously you will be looking to add nine of those to one shovel of cement, adjusting the mix once with additional sand as required. To get an idea of the consistency you are looking for, have a look on Youtube for foundation concrete. Plenty of videos on there will offer the best assistance as to how it should look when mixed correctly. Photographs in a book can only show you so much and watching how the mixture slumps and behaves when mixed correctly is best seen in a video. Keep mixing batches, pouring the concrete into the form and using an old rake or trowel spread it around, pushing it into the corners. You will see how this motion also helps compact the concrete and expel any trapped air, which will weaken the slab if left in.

The aim is for the level of the concrete at this stage to be slightly higher than the top of the frame. Gently tap the wooden form on the sides with a hammer, which will further help to expel any air bubbles still trapped. At this point, get yourself a straight piece of wood that you can hold in your hands and that is just a bit longer than the wooden form. Starting at one end, sit the piece of wood on top of the frame. Now, keeping the wood flat and square with the form and not lifting it, slide it left and right but not too much. At the same time, you should be bringing the wood towards you, working your way across the form. Continue this until you reach the other side of the form. This will give you a roughly smooth surface that can be gently smoothed further if you wish with a trowel or float.

The concrete now needs to chemically 'cure' as opposed to dry, so you don't actually want it to dry out too quickly or the curing process will not work. To achieve this, once the concrete has reached the stage where you can gently press the surface and it doesn't leave a mark, try and cover the foundation slab with some plastic or tarpaulin. Depending on the thickness of the slab, I recommend leaving it for a week or so before removing the plastic and progressing to the next phase of the build.

Chapter 4
The Base

Once the foundation slab is fully cured and solid, we can begin to build the Base, which will hold the oven at a height that we can use and see into easily.

The base can be constructed of any number of things really because it is far enough away from the fire to be a problem, although I still wouldn't personally recommend wood or combustible materials. It is possible though.

Most people opt for building bricks or breeze blocks as in the photograph above. Breeze blocks are cheap in comparison to bricks and can be finished decoratively on the outside in a number of different ways.

The size of the base will of course be governed by the size of your oven, as discussed in Chapter 3 and will use the figures that we looked at in terms of estimating the overall size of your oven including insulation and a decorative finish layer.

Lay the breeze blocks out like jigsaw pieces to see how it will all fit on the foundation slab, bearing in mind how big your hearth needs to be. When thinking about how high to build your base, you need to factor in the finished height of your foundation slab, the base, the planned thickness of your hearth slab and the thickness of your cooking floor. This will be personal to you and those using the oven and will need to be high enough that you are not bending down too much to see into the oven but not so high as to make it difficult or dangerous to handle hot and heavy cooking pans and so forth. As a guide, I am 5 foot 11 and from the ground in front of the oven to the cooking floor is 43 inches or 1092mm.

Once you have determined the layout of your breeze blocks, lay them out accurately, making any cuts you need to with a hand saw or bolster and chisel. This is where the hollow blocks were my favored choice because you can simply mix more of the concrete mix we used for the foundation slab and pour the mix down the hollow holes of the breeze blocks. For added strength, you can drop single lengths of reinforced steel bar down some or all of the holes too. If you are building an open wood storage area and so need to bridge the blocks across, you can use two lengths of 'L' shaped steel across the gap for the suspended blocks to sit on. These types of steel off-cuts can be purchased cheaply from your local steel stockbroker as I discovered.

I also added a 'leg' to the centre of the base, made from blocks in the same way as the walls, as I felt that this would provide more support for the hearth slab and oven.

The base then needs to be left for around a week for the concrete to cure. As with the foundation, it helps to cover the walls with plastic to try and prevent the concrete from drying out too fast.

Chapter 5
The Hearth Slab

At this stage in the build we are starting to get somewhere and with the base built it makes it easier to visualize the height and scale of what the finished oven will look like.

But we have a problem and that comes in the form of a big hole in the centre of the base where we need our oven to sit. What we will now do is pour another slab of concrete similar to the foundation slab only we don't have the ground to pour the slab on. We therefore need to lay something down first that will support the concrete whilst it cures and there are a couple of options here. You can use temporary boards such as plywood sheeting, propped up with makeshift legs for support. These legs and boards will then need to be removed once the hearth slab is cured.

Alternatively, I opted to use cement board which you can purchase from DIY shops and also tile stores as it is used as a backing for fixing tiles to. I used two of these and laid them slightly overlapping the walls.

In the above photo, you can also see that I built a wooden framework to contain the concrete for the hearth slab. This framework can be positioned directly in line with the walls but I wanted the slab to step out from the walls to make it look better so you will see that I added more wood to achieve this. If you wish to add curves to the front or sides of the form this is possible using thinner lengths of wood, bent to whatever shape you wish. Note the legs surrounding the walls, holding the wooden form up. Screws were used to make it easier to dismantle the form once the

concrete had set. More concrete mixing at this stage in exactly the same way as for the foundation slab, making sure that the air is expelled from the mix as you go.

The slab will take around a week before you can move onto the second hearth slab, which sits on top of this one.

So that is the structural hearth slab completed but if we built the oven directly on this then two things would happen. The heat from the oven/cooking floor would leak out, making the oven less efficient at retaining heat but also, the heat would likely damage the standard concrete slab. Over time, this could well cause structural weakness in the slab and in turn the integrity of the oven.

What we must do is put a barrier between the bottom of the oven and this hearth slab in order to prevent any damage or heat loss. This comes in the form of insulation and there are a number of options from glass bottles to expensive ceramic fibreboard - which has the advantage of being so thin that you can simply sit it on top of the structural hearth slab and avoid the need to pour a second slab. I opted instead for lightweight fly-ash building blocks laid on their side as these were inexpensive and easy to install. They also have great insulation properties but the downside is that they were quite large and so needed to be buried in the centre of a second insulating hearth slab. This was always my plan though and so I had factored in the depth of this second hearth slab in terms of my total oven height. Depending on your insulation type though, it is possible to sometimes set your insulation within the structural hearth slab, avoiding the need to pour two separate slabs.

A lot of oven builders opt for vermicrete as their insulating layer. This is a mix of vermiculite, cement and water that we will cover later in the book when it comes to insulating the dome. I didn't use it at the hearth stage though, mainly because it can take a long time to completely dry out and allow the rest of the build to proceed but if time is on your side, maybe consider it?

In the photo above, you can see how I positioned the lightweight blocks in the centre of the structural hearth slab and then surrounded them with more standard concrete to bring everything up to the same level. Note that this insulation is only required where there is heat - under the cooking floor so you need to ensure that the insulation sits under the anticipated footprint of the oven floor.

You will also see that more wooden forms have been built to contain the second concrete pour for the insulating hearth slab.

Chapter 6

The Cooking Floor

I hope that you have been patting yourself on the back up to this point anyway but that is especially true for this part of the build because we are finally ready to start building the oven itself, beginning with the cooking floor.

Firebricks are the usual material of choice for this, even if the rest of your build is in regular brick, because of the superior heat retention properties of firebricks, which will really help to cook those pizzas in record time by ensuring that the heat is directed up into the base at the same time as the flames cooking the toppings.

Firebricks come in all shapes and sizes so you will need to lay yours out in order to work out the correct number required for your cooking floor. It is important to select your very best bricks for this to ensure that the cooking floor is as level and flat as possible as this is the surface that you will be moving the pizza peel over.

Orientation wise - make up your own mind here. Some suggest a herring bone pattern as this is thought to avoid pizza peels catching but I have never encountered a problem in laying the bricks as shown above and this also reduced the need for lots of very accurate cuts that are required for the herring bone design.

A template will really help here. Using the dimensions of my hearth slab, oven size, wall thicknesses and insulation, I drew out a circle template on two large pieces of cardboard. My template circle included the first row of half bricks for the dome walls (called the soldier course). This means that my soldier course sits on top of the cooking floor. Some people prefer instead to have their soldier course sat on the hearth slab with the cooking floor sitting inside of the walls. This has the added advantage of being able to remove and replace broken bricks later down the line but as you can imagine - requires some very accurate cutting to ensure that the outside edge of the cooking floor meets the solider course neatly. That said, if there are gaps between the floor and walls these will quickly fill with ash during use, as will any other minor gaps in the cooking floor so don't worry too much.

Once you have your circular template I recommend laying your bricks out loosely to work out how big your landing area is going to be and how everything is going to fit. Pick out your best bricks for the cooking floor with nice clean edges and of similar sizing. This will make for a good cooking floor from the start. Take your time here, make sure you are happy with the layout and make sure it fits your slab, leaving room for insulation layers, final finishing layers and so forth. Mark out your cuts and get to work crafting the floor into a circle - whether your soldier course is to fit on top of or outside of the cooking floor. If like me, your soldier course is going to sit on top of the floor then the added advantage is that the cooking floor cuts can be rough because they will eventually be buried in the outer layers of the oven. Does it make a difference which way round you do things? In short, no and it's a personal preference as I believe that any heat retention advantage/disadvantage is negligible for amateur purposes.

Fire bricks can be cut using a number of different mechanical cutters or simply a bolster and chisel - which is what I used for the majority of cuts, particularly the half bricks for the dome. Simply mark the brick up and place it on a surface that is not too harsh - I used a grassed lawn.

Progress around all four sides of the brick using the bolster and chisel to gently but reasonably hit the chisel along the cut line. Just one hit at a time before moving the chisel round and striking it again. Continue this process patiently around the brick a number of times until it breaks.

Once you are completely happy with the floor, it needs to be bedded onto the hearth slab with a mix of sand and a little fire clay, ensuring that the bricks are gently tapped into place and level with the surrounding bricks. Take your time and get the floor nice and level.

Chapter 7
The Dome

We are now ready to start building the dome itself and this starts with the soldier course, which is the very first row of bricks and will sit on the edge of the cooking floor or around the outside, depending on your design. This row can be a full brick on its end, a half brick on its side or a half brick on its longer edge - it all just depends what design you have gone for. Obviously a full brick on its end will increase the overall height of the dome. As you can see from the photo above, I opted for half bricks on their edge, just to lift the initial height of the dome.

After that, it was half bricks on their longer edge with the joints staggered. The start and finish of the soldier course butts up against a slightly larger brick that transitions into what will become the base of the arch. Note on the left hand side of the landing area that this transition brick protrudes slightly into the landing area than the brick in front of it. This will provide a 'jam' to butt a door up against and form a nice seal for trapping the heat in!

In this chapter we will focus only on the dome itself but the next chapter will explain the construction of the oven entrance including the arches and how these tie in with the dome.

For instructions on how to cut the bricks, see the previous chapter.

Sticking the bricks together

Regular mortar won't cut it here. Eventually, the heat of the oven will burn off the cement and all you will be left with is sand and water, which is not enough to keep your oven from collapsing into itself. You can buy ready-mixed 'air set' mortars in big tubs but you will find two problems with these. First, they are expensive and you will use a lot of them. Second is that you will usually find that they state they are not suitable to use in gaps that are more than a few mm wide. Some of the joints in the oven's construction will indeed be just a few mm wide but as you will find, there are other areas where you need a product that is suitable for use in much wider gaps. The answer to this problem is to mix your own special mortar that has come to be known as 'Homebrew'. It is a mix of sand, cement, fireclay, lime and water. The sand, cement and water act in the same way as a traditional mortar but the additional of the fireclay and lime means that even when the cement has burnt away over time, your oven will still hold together for hopefully many years to come. What this concoction provides is a mortar that is very sticky which you will be thankful for when the rows of your dome progress and you are tasked with trying to stick bricks in a position so upright that with a normal mortar they would simply slide off and onto the floor. That is where the 'indispensable tool' comes in but more on that in a minute.

The homebrew can be used for the entire dome in tight gaps or great big ones. It can even be spread over the outside of the dome as you go, to hold everything in place even better, as you can see in the above photo. This is optional however and some of you will prefer to have the outside of the dome looking just as good as the inside - especially if you decide not to add any insulation. So what is the recipe? Well, this will be governed slightly by your materials. Some sand has a higher water content and fireclays can be different too so although I have set out a base recipe below, be prepared to adjust things slightly if you find that the mix is too dry or too wet. As with a normal mortar, you mix the dry ingredients first and then add water gradually to create that sticky homebrew. When mixed properly, you will be able to scoop it onto a brick-laying trowel, turn it upside down and it will just cling to the trowel, showing no sign of moving! Make sure it isn't too dry though, you want it slightly wet or the mix will begin to dry before you have all of your bricks laid and you cannot resurrect a drying homebrew by adding water so dont try! Having said that, the fire clay can cause the homebrew to dry out and crack as it dries so I found that having a spray bottle and misting the homebrew/newly laid bricks periodically with water helped to reduce the cracking. If it really becomes a problem, consider placing cling film over the newly laid bricks whist the homebrew dries in order to remain the moisture level.

Soaking the bricks in a bucket of water for a few minutes before laying them can also help to prevent them sucking the moisture from the homebrew too quickly as fire bricks are very porous.

Mix the homebrew in small batches and you will soon learn how many bricks you can lay with each mix so that you can have the bricks cut and ready, including the last brick in the chain which will always be an odd size and should fit tightly against the larger brick that transitions to the base of the arch that is referred to above.

As you lay the bricks, carefully try to clean the face of the brick that will sit inside the oven with clean water. Removing excess homebrew at this stage is a lot easy than waiting for it to dry!

Homebrew:

I cut down a sports water bottle to help with measuring and found that the following ratios provided a good mix, although as I said - each set of materials is different. Other ratios can also be found online so there may be some experimenting before you achieve the right consistency.

Traditionally, the mix is around 3.1.1.1 in that you should be using 3 sand to one of everything else but I found that just didn't work for me.

1.5 scoops of red building sand, Half a scoop of cement, Half a scoop of lime, A quarter of a scoop of fire clay

The Indispensable tool

I said I would come back to this. As you build the walls of the dome, you must set the bricks at an angle. This angle of course has to be correct if the sides of the dome are to eventually come together at the top and close the dome neatly. To assist with this, many oven builders including myself used an indispensable tool, which can be seen in the above photograph at the start of the chapter. Very simply, it is an arm that is anchored in some way to the very centre of the cooking floor. This fixing point must allow the arm to rotate around the oven and also be hinged so that the arm can move up and down. For my version I in fact used nothing more than a hinge with a loose screw in it. At the other end of the arm is a small right-angled bracket, which should sit neatly but not too tightly against the corner of the soldier brick course. When laying each row of bricks, the arm of the indispensable tool can be swung into place to almost meet the new brick, not to support it but so that you can match the right-angle of the bracket with the top edge of the new brick, adding or taking away homebrew from underneath the brick in order to achieve the correct angle before moving onto the next brick. There are other ways of forming the dome such as filling the space with sand, laying the bricks against it and then removing the sand. Alternatively, some people opt to build multiple 'D' shapes out of wood, foam or cardboard, slotting them together and using them as a guide for the dome's curve. Once the dome is built and has dried, these supports are then usually broken and removed through the entrance to the oven.

For the last few rows of the dome, you will find that even homebrew needs a helping hand to keep the bricks in place while everything sets. At this point, you may find that progress slows as you are forced to lay just a couple of bricks at a time, propping each one up at its correct angle with the use of temporary props or clamps. I opted for a slightly different approach in that I constructed a wooden platform the same diameter as the remaining hole of the dome.

This platform had to be made up of several pieces of wood screwed together so that it could be dismantled and taken out through the front opening of the oven when finished. The platform was propped from underneath so that the platform was almost level with the last row of bricks. I used a bucket for this, which I don't recommend as it collapsed - fortunately after everything had set so it didn't cause a problem but my advice is to use something stronger as a prop! Onto the platform, I then added red building sand and formed a large sandcastle to the same curvature as the dome. This then allowed me to continue with the last rows of the build, with each brick resting on the sand for its angle. The theory is that as the rows or rings of bricks go higher and smaller, the bricks should all be cut smaller so that the last brick is one neatly cut 'keystone' that locks everything into place. If you have the skills to cut and craft such a closure to the oven then great but I opted for an easier method which was to simply fill the final small hole in the top of the dome with off-cuts of fire brick, resting against the sand. For any gaps, I would add smaller fragments of brick before covering the whole dome with homebrew, pushing it in between and around all of the small bricks and gaps, creating a tightly compact dome top. I left this for around a week to dry before removing the support (taking out the collapsed bucket!).

Once the dome has had time to dry, you can then add homebrew to the joints on the inside of the oven, 'pointing' everything up and then doing a final clean with clean water and a sponge.

Chapter 8
The Entrance

This is the sight that every oven builder dreams of. That small, brick-framed window that allows you to see into the heart of the oven and watch the flames dance and the food sizzle.

In the last chapter we focused on the dome but as it rises, so too must the entrance as the walls tie in with the start and finish of each brick ring of the dome. We mentioned previously, the transition brick that sits at the end of each row in the dome and you can see them in the above photo. Three on either side, towards the back of the entrance and protruding slightly into the landing area to enable our door to butt up against them. In front of them are the walls of the entrance. Note how the fifth brick has been cut into a wedge shape to allow either side of the arch to sit on the walls.

Once the walls have been built, you can measure the gap that you have to fill with the arch. I recommend that you transfer this measurement to a small sheet of plywood or similar and then lay out the bricks in order to establish the curve required so that not only does the arch sit on each side of the walls but that the bricks all touch on the lower edge. If this proves to be a problem, consider cutting an irregular, central keystone to sit in the middle of the arch in order to fill the gap and ensure a tight fit of the bricks.

Next, cut out the arch to include an area beneath it as shown in the following photograph, which shows the construction of the rear arch. The template should not sit on the cooking floor but should be temporarily propped up. This makes the template much easier to drop down and remove when the arch is set. Two identical templates sandwiched between small lengths of batten ensure that the bricks of the arch sit securely on the template. Homewbrew can then be added and pushed firmly in between the uppermost gaps between the bricks, pointing the front and top joints as required. Leave for a short while before carefully wiping off any excess homebrew from the front of the brick. The arch should then be left for around a week to completely harden.

The front arch is built in exactly the same way but where the arch meets, it is necessary to create a hole that will be used for the chimney. On an oven this size, a 6 inch diameter flue is used for the chimney and so the hole you create in this front arch needs to be as large as possible when the flue sits on top. You can probably see that this hole was created by cutting two outer bricks into 'C' shapes with a quarter brick at the front and back of the arch acting as keystones.

Note that the brick that can be seen sitting in the hole in the photo below is merely supporting the curing arch and was removed afterwards.

Tying the rear arch into the rows of the dome is relatively straight forward but we now come to a tricky point in the build in that we now need to close the gap where the oven entrance is so that our final rows of the dome will be complete circles. This requires finding a way of sitting a handful of half bricks on top of the rear arch, at an angle that will match the next row in the dome's construction and allow you to lay the first complete row of bricks in a full circle in the dome.

The following two photographs will hopefully show you what this looks like by showing you what the inside of the dome looked like with just the arch and then the next photo shows the three bricks in place. These bricks had small notches cut into them to allow them to sit over the arch. Homebrew was applied and the bricks carefully propped whilst this section dried.

The result was not as circular as I would have liked but this was rectified in the subsequent rows. The technique worked though although you may well be able to come up with a better solution with your own build. This completes the main structure of the entrance and hopefully explains how it and the dome are constructed with reference to the previous chapter.

Chapter 9
The Chimney

The chimney is an important part of the oven and is not for simply removing the smoke from the oven, as you may think.

During operation of the oven, the chimney will actually help the fire in the oven to burn better and more efficiently. How it does this is buried in physics but we simply need to understand that you will need around a 1 meter flue or around 5-6 inches in diameter. This may seem pretty big but the long length of the flu is needed for it to perform at its best. Shorter, more subtle chimneys can be installed but you will notice that the fire will struggle to get going. Of more annoyance will be that the smoke from the oven is likely to simply drift out of the oven door and into your face. An oven with a longer, taller flue may do this initially whilst the flue is heating up but once it is hot, you will see that any smoke from the oven is largely wicked straight up the chimney and away, due to what is known as the chimney's 'draw'.

Having a chimney with a 1 meter flue may be great during the oven's operation but the downside can be that it looks a little unsightly when the oven is simply a garden ornament. It can also be a hindrance if you wish to ever cover the oven to protect it from the elements.

Some people are perfectly happy to live with this but if not, there is a solution. The flue can be installed in two pieces, comprising of a short socket section that is permanently attached to the oven and then a longer, removable piece that is only fitted when the oven is being used.

The flue can be made of different materials although the design I will show you is a simple single-walled flue, which as the name implies is just one sheet of metal rolled into a tube. Twin-walled flues can be used in the alternative and these have the advantage of being hot on the inside but cooler on the outside due to them being comprised of two layers of metal with insulation between. The removable socket design that I will explain could be used with a twin walled system using slightly different components but is likely to be more expensive.

For the single-walled flue, I purchased a 1 meter length of enamel flue with a 6 inch diameter, fairly inexpensively from ebay. One end of the flue has a rolled lip a little way from the end and this is going to be the top of our short permanent section that is always attached to the oven. Using an angle grinder, carefully cut this end off the overall length of the flue. The exact size will be determined by how much of the socket you wish to be showing when the larger section of flue is not attached. In the following photos, you will see that I allowed for building a section, decorative arch and short brick chimney around the base of this section, which is required in order to properly anchor this short piece in place.

To the cut end of this short section, I then used the angle grinder to make small evenly-spaced cuts and then bent these out to form tabs, hammering them gently on a flat surface. The chimney was then placed over the hole in the arch and the tabs adjusted to achieve a good fit. I then used a high temperature sealant spread all over the tabs in order to close any gaps and bond it with the arch.

You can see from the photo above that at this stage I had already added a second, decorative arch in normal brick, over the firebrick arch and this allowed me to gauge the length of the short flue section required. Once the sealant had cured, the remainder of the decorative arch was completed, making sure that a gap was left around the flue.

To this, I opted to add a further short brick stack to help anchor the short flue section in place. If you do this, be sure to leave a gap around the flue again.

This gap was then filled with vermicrete, which will be used later to insulate the oven. It is comprised of vermiculate, cement and water. Vermiculate looks like a small aggregate gravel although is extremely light. It has many different uses, particularly in gardening but it also has excellent insulating properties which is why it is ideal for packing around the chimney section in order to act as a barrier between the hot flue and the surrounding brick support.

Once filled with vermiculate, the top of the chimney stack around the flue can be sealed using refractory cement or the homebrew mixture again in order to cover and protect the fragile vermicrete from the elements. It is a good idea to allow an expansion gap around the flue, rather than have the homebrew touch the flue. The reason for this is that the flue will expand and contract during use and the homebrew will not like this as it has no such flexible properties and is likely to simply crack. Leaving a small gap and then filling it with a suitable, flexible, high temperature product is best. Have a look at how wood burning stove flues are sealed in order to decide which option is best for your design as there are different considerations to factor in.

We now have our short, fixed section with the rolled lip at the top and so need to make our longer, removable section. For this, I purchased a matching diameter socket section that is able to accept the flue into either side of it. It was then simply a question of pushing the socket onto the longer length of the flue over the cut end. This sat quite tight and no additional sealant was required.

Prior to the oven being lit, this socket section and long length of flue is then simply lifted onto and slotted over the short fixed length of flue on the oven. Both sections grip tightly during use as the metal expands, forming a tight seal between them. Once cooled, both pieces return to their original size and the longer section is able to be easily lifted from the oven and stored in a shed out of the way. This last photo shows the full flue in place and you can clearly see the silver socket section that forms the join. A rain cap can be added if required. When not in use, a simple cover over the short socket section will prevent rain from dripping soot onto your oven landing and I use a small up-turned terra-cotta dish.

Chapter 10
Insulation

The fire bricks that we used for the walls of the dome will retain the heat from the fire for hours - even long after the fire itself has gone out. The aim in adding insulation though is to trap this heat for even longer and it is this that makes it possible to cook for long periods of time without having to constantly maintain a significant fire inside the oven.

The amount and thickness of your insulation will depend on your design, your budget and what you have room for on your hearth slab. Add as much insulation as you can as this will retain the oven's heat for longer and ensure that you get the most from the different types of cooking including overnight slow roasts of meat.

Below, I shall describe the two types of insulation that are applied to my oven but other options are available and there is no set rule other than the more insulation the better and that any insulation is generally better than no insulation! If you can only stretch to one layer of insulation though because of space or financial consideration - just add that and don't worry, it will still help the oven retain heat a little better.

The first layer of my oven is wrapped with insulating blanket called Superwool Plus fibre but other options are available with various thicknesses and specifications. I opted for 25mm thickness purely on cost but go for a little more if you can stretch to it. Be careful what you buy though and do a little research first. Some insulation blankets are more hazardous than others and are actually being phased out I understand, though are usually only an issue during handling so just be careful if using those products and always read the data sheets with them for advice.

The blanket is easy to cut and can simply be wrapped around the oven over the brick dome, cutting smaller pieces to ensure that none of the dome is showing and you have a nice tight layer all over.

The addition of chicken wire is simply to make it easier to add the next layer although some people do not bother with this. If you decide to, it is just a question of wrapping the wire around and over the dome, twisting it together where it meets in order to create a tight layer stretched over the dome.

Vermicrete

Over the top of the blanket, you can add a layer of vermicrete which we referred to in Chapter 9 during the construction of the chimney. Vermicrete is a mix of vermiculite, cement and water and the ratio is anywhere between 5-10 parts of vermiculite to 1 part of cement, with water added in stages until it clumps together. I found that a mix ratio of 8:1 worked best.

Be warned, this is tricky stuff to mix as it is very light so forget about doing it on a windy day! The water will also not be very well absorbed by the mixture so don't add too much, it just needs to be able to clump together.

Using gloved hands or a trowel, transfer the mix to the dome and begin building from the bottom of the dome all around, before then starting to work your way up the sides, building on the vermicrete until you have a layer of the stuff all over the dome and none of the blanket can be seen. This layer can be built up gradually and should be at least 2-3 inches thick and preferably more if you have the space on the hearth slab. Don't worry if the vermiculite is brittle and keeps falling off - this is normal and you should just continue to carefully add it, filling in any gaps gradually and trying to form a nice albeit rough dome shape. When finished, I added a fine sprinkling of cement over the entire dome and then misted lightly with a spray bottle, which helped to hold everything in place.

Leave the dome for several days or until it firms up depending on how thick you applied it. Loosely cover the dome whilst it is hardening if you wish to protect it from the rain and weather.

Chapter 11
Curing the Oven

With the insulation on, its time to light our first fire. Wait I hear you shout - the oven isn't finished, well that's exactly why we are lighting a fire. I'll explain, you see during the process of building the dome up to this point we have used a fair amount of water. Water in the homebrew mix and water in the vermiculite if that was used. If we applied a finishing layer to the oven now and then tried to throw a pizza party with our first light of the oven, it is likely that you would be forced to sit around eating take away pizza, staring at a broken oven with great big cracks in it. Why? because the heat would turn the water that is trapped in the oven to steam and that steam would then want to escape by breaking through the final, sealed layer of your nice oven!
What we have to do is therefore encourage this trapped water to work its way out of the oven whilst it still has a relatively easy way out. Some people even have a few small fires before even adding the insulation and then have yet more fires before adding the final finishing layer of the dome.

Unfortunately, there is no scientific formula for calculating the temperature and duration of these 'curing' fires but you should aim to start slow and steady. Maybe light and maintain a small fire for an hour or so and then let it go out and the oven cool. Then perhaps later in the day or the following day, light another fire - same size but keep it going a little longer. The point is to just very slowly increase the size of the fire and the length of time that you maintain it in order to force all of that excess water out. Curing fires should take around a week or so before you even think about using the oven to cook in. Even then, you still want to build the size and duration of fires rather than just go from curing fires one day to raging inferno the next.

A shorter version of this process should also be adopted following a long spell of the oven not being used such as over the winter for example. This is because moisture from the general atmosphere can soak into the oven and it needs to be driven out again before trying to run the oven at those temperatures required for pizza and roasting. That said, some recipes actually require lower temperatures of course and so feel free to incorporate some gentle cooking during the curing process if you can.

Some general tips for fire building are to always use dry, seasoned wood from a reputable source. Scrap bits of wood, pallets, furniture etc should not be burnt in an oven which will be used for cooking food as they can give off potentially harmful chemicals from preservatives, paint, varnishes etc that have been added to the wood.

Always aim to build a new fire towards the front of the dome where it will benefit from increased air. Once established, it can be pushed back into the middle of the oven.

Finally, you can build what is termed as an upside down fire and this technique ensures that the fire builds quickly and burns efficiently with minimal smoke. Larger pieces of wood sit at the bottom with progressively smaller pieces all the way up to the top, ending with a couple of natural wax fire lighters on top. Light these and the fire will catch from the top to the bottom as it builds. Newspaper is not required and usually just creates a mess in my opinion.

Chapter 12

Structural and Decorative finishes

<u>Dome</u>

Once the curing process is finished it is time to add the final layer to the oven. This will protect the delicate insulation from the weather and allow us to make the oven look nice as a general feature.

Different options are available here ranging from mosaic tiles to a simple render. I applied a render as it is the most straightforward. Tarmac produce a one coat render which is what I used and I used around four 25kg bags to cover the oven and the base. It is easy to use and apply and can be gently polished with a wet sponge when still wet to achieve a relatively smooth finish. This process closes the surface of the render to keep the weather out.

On the corners of the base, I rounded them off roughly then used clout nails and adhesive to attach narrow lengths of plastering mesh for the render to bond to. Plasters bead was also attached towards the bottom of the walls to try and avoid water wicking up from the floor and into the render.

Once dry, use a good masonry paint like Sandtex and apply a couple of coats.

<u>Second Arch</u>

I decided to add a second arch around the firebrick arch. This was mainly decorative but does serve to add support to both the entrance walls and also the short length of flue that sits above the entrance. I used normal bricks for this but opted for the homebrew still given that the bricks are still exposed to some heat during use.

Hearth

Most people opt to tile the hearth just to improve its appearance. I decided to go for a mosaic effect using some old bathroom tiles that I happened to have. I just took a hammer to them and then fixed/grouted them with an all in one mix that is actually designed for swimming pools so I thought it would fare well in the British weather. It comes as a dry mix and water is simply added.

Chapter 13
The Door

Whenever there is a live fire in the oven you will not want to close the door completely - not unless you want the fire to go out that is. However, when you just have glowing embers remaining or perhaps when you have raked the fire out and the oven is still warm, then a door is helpful in trapping the heat inside. It also creates a more stable environment for say baking because you no longer have air coming into the oven through the entrance. If you decide to have a go at overnight slow roasts in your oven then a door is particularly useful in preventing the neighborhood wildlife from getting their hands on the cooked joint of meat before you wake up! If you are using the oven on a particularly windy day, a half-open door in the entrance can help to shield the fire from the wind whilst also allowing air in to feed the fire. Finally, I also find it useful to use a door simply when the oven is not in use in order to prevent debris, pets or anything else finding its way into the oven!

Doors come in two styles generally - insulated and non-insulated. Adding insulation to a door is preferred but a little trickier to achieve in that you have to find a material that is able to stand up to the high temperatures of the inside of the oven. It also has to be robust and not chip easily when being moved around and able to fix handles to. That is quite a shopping list and most people deal with this by building a facing sheet to the door that will sit outside of the oven and have handles. They then attach insulation material to the back. Alternatively, some people build a thick hollow door that has the insulation encapsulated within it. Others (like me) just opt for a basic non-insulating door!

An insulated door is clearly better but as with everything in a build of this nature you will find that you have to know your limitations and work within them. I can't fabricate metal to such a degree and I cannot afford to pay someone to build a door for me so that's simply where things stand. Another option though is to purchase a new or second hand oven door (usually made from cast iron) before building the oven and entrance. Using the measurements from the door you can then build your oven to fit the door, rather than the other way around.

To make my oven door, I first visited a local steelworks for a simple square off cut of a piece of sheet metal - strong enough to support itself well but not so heavy that I would need to crane it into place every time. Know what you are buying too - don't opt for galvanized metal for instance as although it looks great, it can give off some nasty chemicals when heated. Taking measurements and templates from the oven opening between the front arch support walls, I transferred this to the sheet metal and carefully cut the shape out using an angle grinder. The edges were sanded once a good fit with the oven opening had been achieved. Don't forget to allow some free movement between the top/bottom and left/right of the door for a small amount of heat expansion during use - you don't want to find that the door has jammed itself into the opening with the heat of the oven and your food is trapped inside!

Handles can be insulated or not. I opted for metal ones on the basis that I always use welder's gauntlets around the oven anyway, assuming that everything can get hot during use. My handles are actually right-angled, cast iron bookshelf supports, which has the added advantage or being able to serve has both handles and also legs to hold the door upright. To attach them, I simply drilled holes and used nuts and bolts to secure. This produces a basic oven door to use with your completed oven.

Chapter 14
Cooking

The aim of this book was primarily to break down the construction process but I felt that I had to include a chapter on actually using the oven!

People often ask me what else you can cook in a wood-fired oven apart from pizza and the answer is - anything! That's right most recipes that use a domestic oven can usually be applied to a wood fired oven. The trick is in learning to use your oven and managing its temperature and this does take a little time.

You will quickly learn though, how long it takes to get the oven to a certain temperature and how to keep it there. Practice moving the fire to the back and sides of the oven once established and see how this affects the temperatures. Using an instant read digital thermometer can really help here. Remember to take readings from the walls and flooring in order to build up a picture of the temperature of the oven overall. For instance, before cooking pizza you want the fire in the centre of the oven in order to heat the floor up. You then need to move the fire to the back or side of the oven and allow the floor in the centre of the oven to drop slightly or you will burn the pizza! Add logs to the fire throughout though in order to maintain a strong frame licking up and across the roof of the oven to cook the top of the pizza. Yum!

Let the oven cool a little further and then maintain a small but steady fire or pile of glowing embers and you can go in with roasts meats, trays of vegetables and the like.

Once the roast is out, let the fire die down and then just before you sit down to eat you can put a baked desert in the very entrance of the oven just to gently cook it through. Turn it halfway through and by the time you have finished your main course your hot desert will be bubbling away and ready to serve.

Of course, this just gives you an idea of the sort of cooking that you can do in the oven and as your experience grows you will discover endless recipes and bakes that lend themselves to being cooked in your wood fired oven. Add a raised grill above or near to glowing embers and you can even grill just as you would on a bbq. A thin layer of ash under the grill will also help to catch any dripping grease and save your nice cooking floor.

In order to get the most from the oven it is a good idea to plan ahead before you light a fire. Think about what you can cook at the various stages of the oven's heat up and cool down process so that none of that energy is wasted. This doesn't have to be food that will be eaten right away but can be pasta sauces and other dishes to cook, cool and even freeze for another time.

Chapter 15
Tools

A quick word about the basic tools you will need to get you started once your oven is built. You will of course add to these as time goes by but it will hopefully give you a little guidance on where to spend money initially;

- A pizza peel - for the obvious pizza cooking but these paddles can also be useful to balance logs on in order to drop them onto the fire at the back of the oven and also for cleaning out the ashes in the oven once it has completely cooled.
- Heavy duty oven gloves/welders gauntlets. Domestic ones will not do here. Go for gloves with fingers rather than mittens for additional dexterity.
- A long handled brush/scraper - for cleaning the oven floor and moving the fire around. Replace this brush when it shows signs of becoming worn as the metal bristles can become loose.
- An infrared thermometer for safe, accurate temperature reading at a safe distance.
- A metal bucket for putting ashes into - always wait until the ashes have cooled if possible before taking them out of the oven.

- An axe for chopping wood.

- A small poker/rake for moving individual logs around in managing the fire.

- A selection of cookware suitable for roasting and baking. Cast iron if possible.

52449342R00030